BASS PLAY-ALONG

AUDIO ACCESS INCLUDED

ERICCLAPTON

PLAYBACK+
Speed • Pitch • Balance • Loop

To access audio visit:
www.halleonard.com/mylibrary

5788-0194-9061-1929

ISBN 978-1-4234-8216-1

Visit Hal Leonard Online at
www.halleonard.com

Contact us:
Hal Leonard
7777 West Bluemound Road
Milwaukee, WI 53213
Email: info@halleonard.com

In Europe, contact:
Hal Leonard Europe Limited
42 Wigmore Street
Marylebone, London, W1U 2RN
Email: info@halleonardeurope.com

In Australia, contact:
Hal Leonard Australia Pty. Ltd.
4 Lentara Court
Cheltenham, Victoria, 3192 Australia
Email: info@halleonard.com.au

CONTENTS

BASS NOTATION LEGEND

Bass music can be notated two different ways: on a *musical staff,* and in *tablature*

THE MUSICAL STAFF shows pitches and rhythms and is divided by bar lines into measures. Pitches are named after the first seven letters of the alphabet.

TABLATURE graphically represents the bass fingerboard. Each horizontal line represents a string, and each number represents a fret.

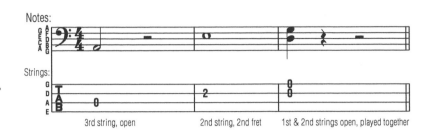

3rd string, open   2nd string, 2nd fret   1st & 2nd strings open, played together

HAMMER-ON: Strike the first (lower) note with one finger, then sound the higher note (on the same string) with another finger by fretting it without picking.

PULL-OFF: Place both fingers on the notes to be sounded. Strike the first note and without picking, pull the finger off to sound the second (lower) note.

LEGATO SLIDE: Strike the first note and then slide the same fret-hand finger up or down to the second note. The second note is not struck.

SHIFT SLIDE: Same as legato slide, except the second note is struck.

TRILL: Very rapidly alternate between the notes indicated by continuously hammering on and pulling off.

TREMOLO PICKING: The note is picked as rapidly and continuously as possible.

VIBRATO: The string is vibrated by rapidly bending and releasing the note with the fretting hand.

SHAKE: Using one finger, rapidly alternate between two notes on one string by sliding either a half-step above or below.

NATURAL HARMONIC: Strike the note while the fret hand lightly touches the string directly over the fret indicated.

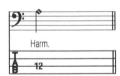

MUFFLED STRINGS: A percussive sound is produced by laying the fret hand across the string(s) without depressing them and striking them with the pick hand.

BEND: Strike the note and bend up the interval shown.

BEND AND RELEASE: Strike the note and bend up as indicated, then release back to the original note. Only the first note is struck.

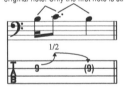

RIGHT-HAND TAP: Hammer ("tap") the fret indicated with the "pick-hand" index or middle finger and pull off to the note fretted by the fret hand.

LEFT-HAND TAP: Hammer ("tap") the fret indicated with the "fret-hand" index or middle finger.

SLAP: Strike ("slap") string with right-hand thumb.

POP: Snap ("pop") string with right-hand index or middle finger.

Additional Musical Definitions

(accent) • Accentuate note (play it louder)

(accent) • Accentuate note with great intensity

(staccato) • Play the note short

D.S. al Coda • Go back to the sign (%), then play until the measure marked ***"To Coda"***, then skip to the section labelled ***"Coda."***

Fill • Label used to identify a brief pattern which is to be inserted into the arrangement.

• Repeat measures between signs.

• When a repeated section has different endings, play the first ending only the first time and the second ending only the second time.

After Midnight

Words and Music by J.J. Cale

Fill 1

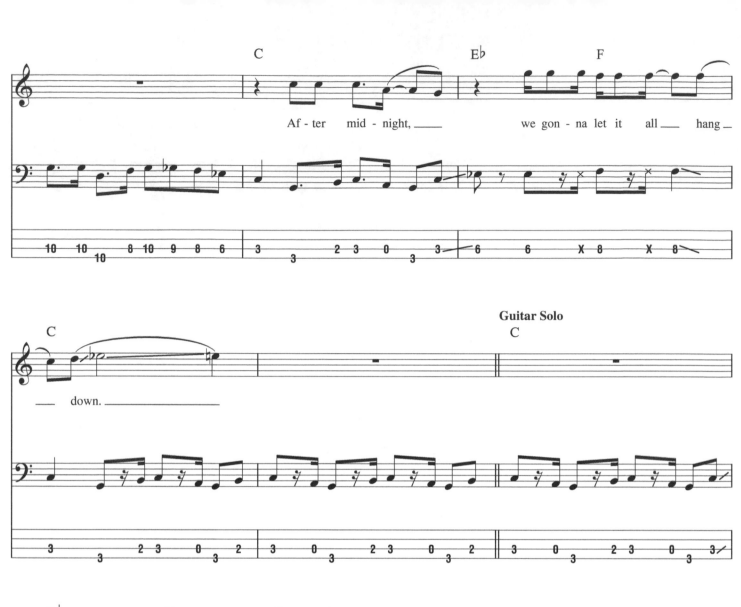

Af - ter mid - night,____ we gon - na let it all___ hang___

____ down._____

Guitar Solo

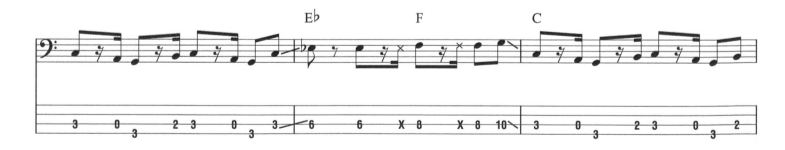

Verse

3. Af - ter mid - night, _____ we're gon - na let it all ___ hang ___

D.S. al Coda

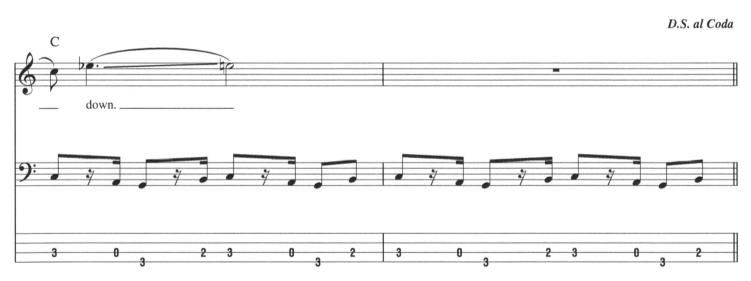

___ down. _____

Coda

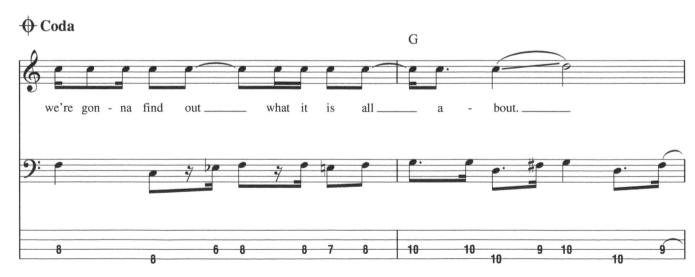

we're gon - na find out _____ what it is all _____ a - bout. _____

Outro

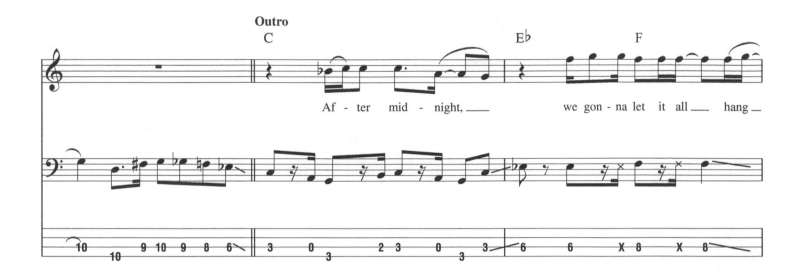

Af - ter mid - night, ____ we gon - na let it all ___ hang __

__ down. _____ Af - ter mid - night, ___

Repeat and fade

we gon' let it all __ hang ___ down. _____

Additional Lyrics

2., 3. After midnight, we're gonna shake your tambourine.
After midnight, it's all gonna be peaches and cream.
We're gonna cause talk and suspicion.
We're gonna give an exhibition.
We're gonna find out what it's all about.

I'm Tore Down

Words and Music by Sonny Thompson

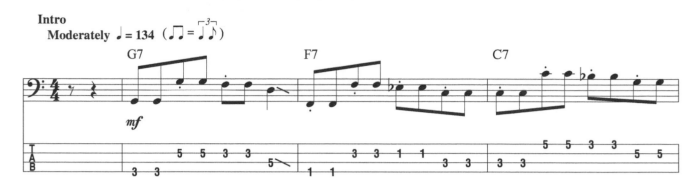

Intro
Moderately ♩ = 134

Chorus

I'm tore down. I'm al-most lev-el with the

ground. ___ I'm tore down. ___ I'm

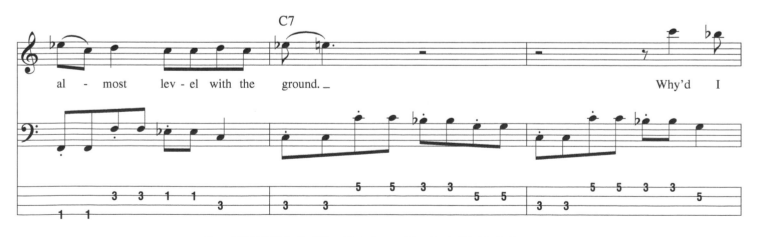

al-most lev-el with the ground. ___ Why'd I

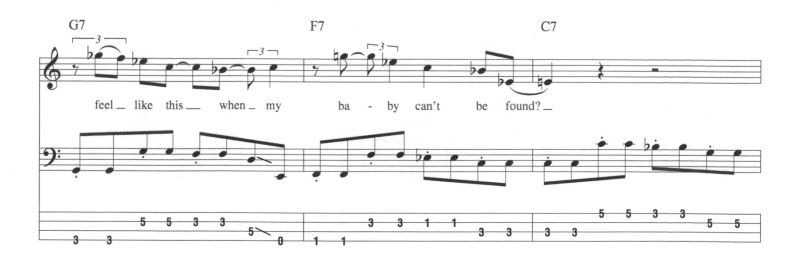

feel _ like this _ when _ my ba - by can't be found? _

Verse

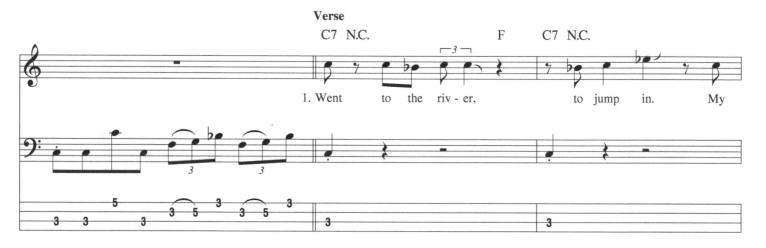

1. Went to the riv - er, to jump in. My

Chorus

ba - by showed up and said, "I will tell you when." Well, I'm tore down,

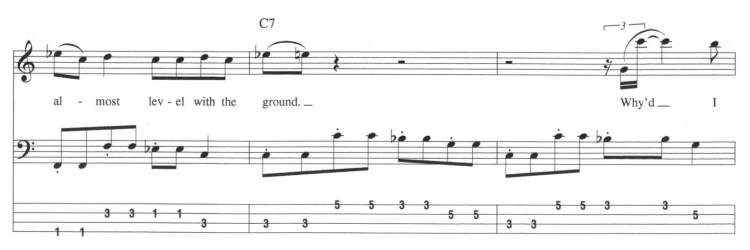

al - most lev - el with the ground. _ Why'd _ I

feel _ like this _ when _ my ba - by can't be found? _

%. **Verse**

2. I love you, babe, _ with all my heart _ and soul. _
3. *See additional lyrics*

2nd time, substitute Fill 1

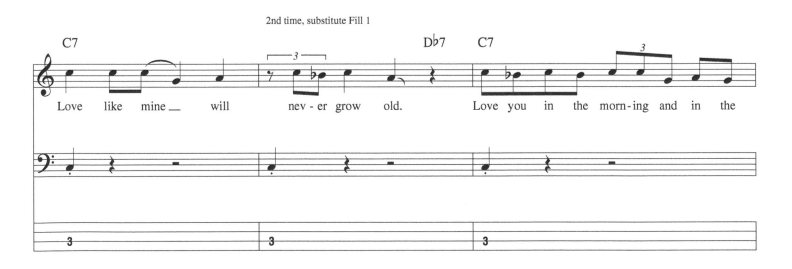

Love like mine _ will nev - er grow old. Love you in the morn-ing and in the

Fill 1

C°7 C N.C.

eve - ning too. __ Ev - 'ry time you leave me I get mad __ with you. __ Well, I'm

Chorus

F7 C7

tore down. __ I'm al - most lev - el with the ground. __

2nd time, substitute Fill 2

G7

Why'd _____ I feel __ like this _____ when __ my

Fill 2

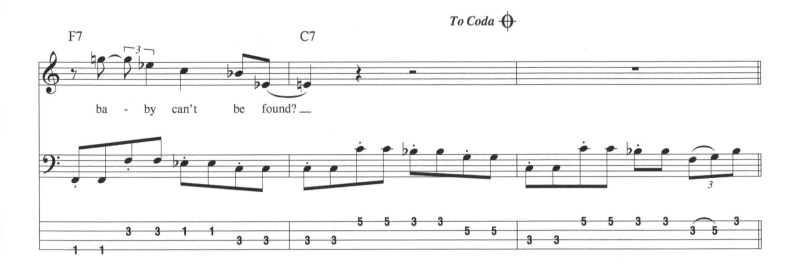

ba - by can't be found? ___

Guitar Solo

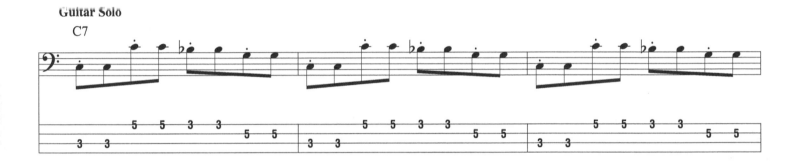

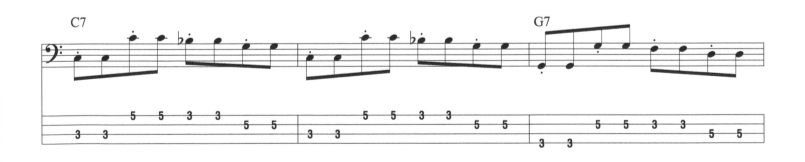

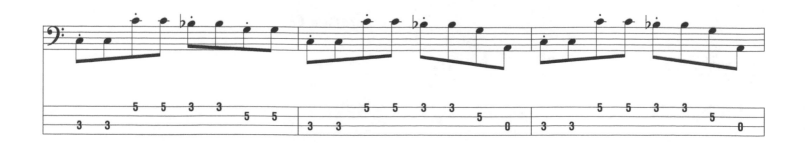

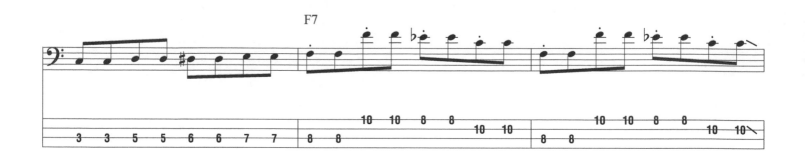

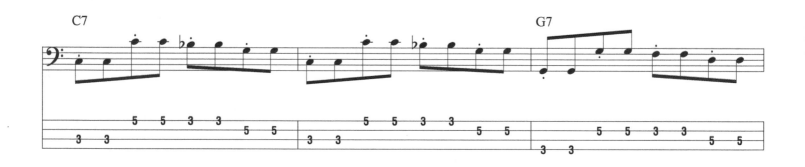

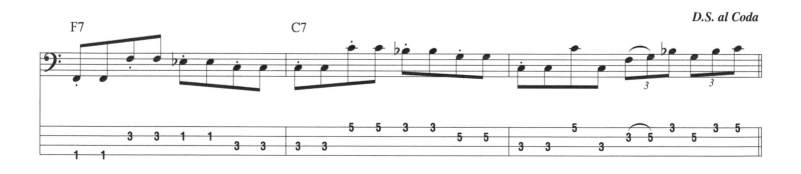

D.S. al Coda

Coda

Outro-Chorus

C7

I'm   tore   down, ____   al - most   lev - el   with   the

ground. _   Well, I'm   tore   down. _   I'm

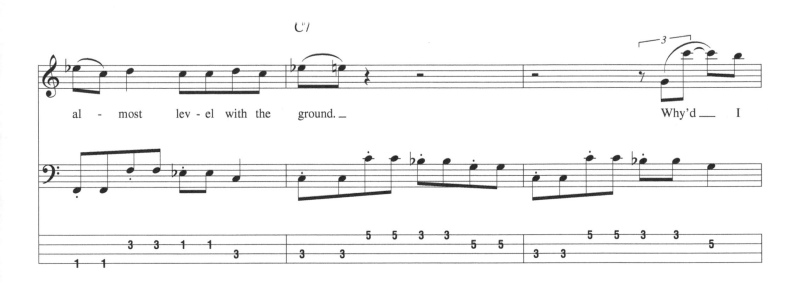

al - most   lev - el   with   the   ground. _   Why'd _ I

feel _ like   this _ when _ my   ba - by   can't   be   found? _

Additional Lyrics

3. Love you, baby, with all my might.
   Love like mine is outta sight.
   I'll lie for you if you want me to.
   I really don't believe that your love is true.

Cocaine

Words and Music by J. J. Cale

When your day is done, and ya wan-na run, co-caine.

She don't lie, ___ she don't lie, ___ she don't like, ___ co-caine. ___

Guitar Solo

3. If   your   thing   is   gone,   and   you

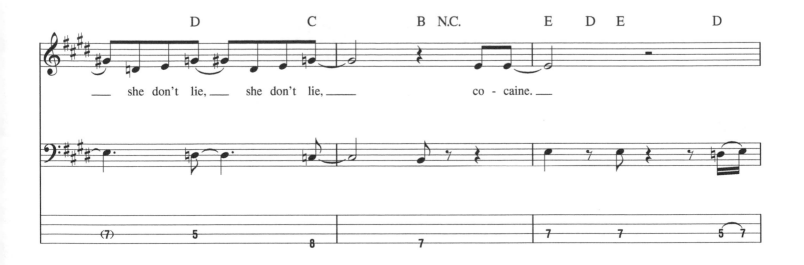

she don't lie, ___ she don't lie, ___ co - caine. ___

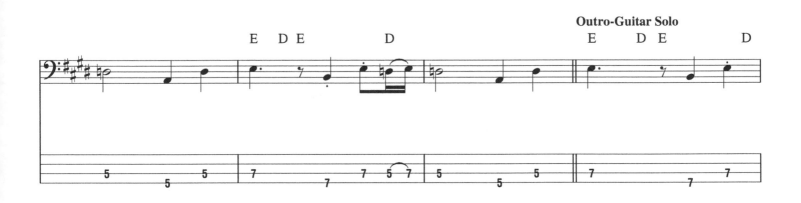

Outro-Guitar Solo

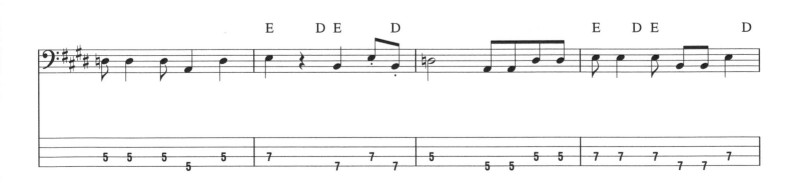

Begin fade

Fade out

Forever Man

Words and Music by Jerry Lynn Williams

Drop D tuning:
(low to high) D-A-D-G

Intro
Moderate Rock ♩ = 112

Verse

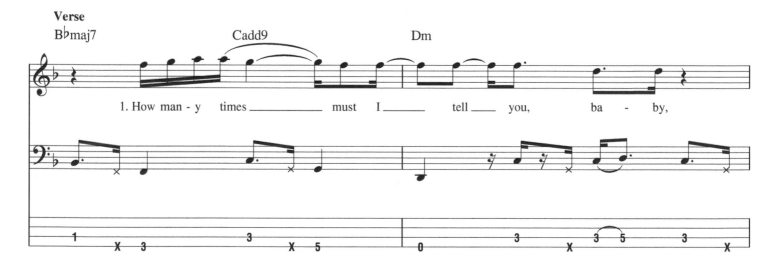

1. How man-y times _____ must I _____ tell _____ you, ba - by,

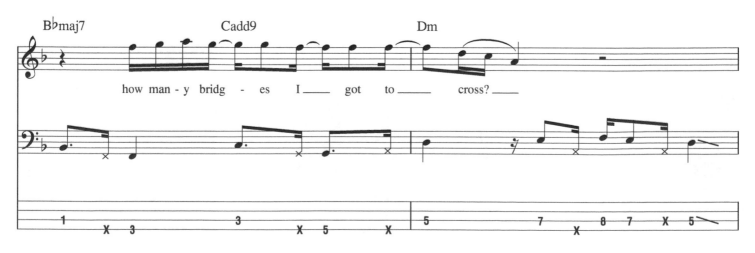

how man-y bridg - es I ___ got to _____ cross? ___

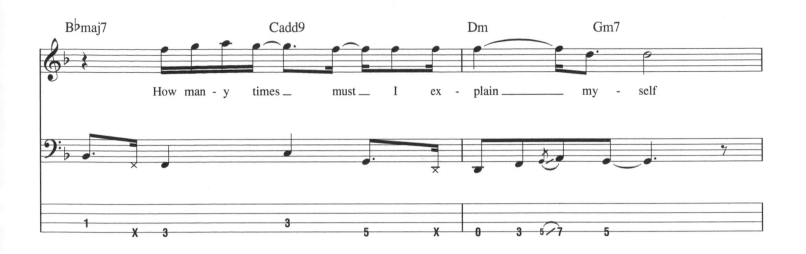

How man - y times ___ must ___ I ex - plain ___ my - self

'fore ___ I can ___ talk ___ to the boss, ___

'fore ___ I can ___ talk to the boss? ___

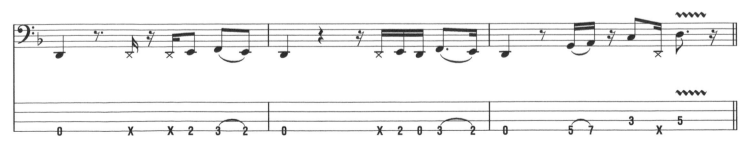

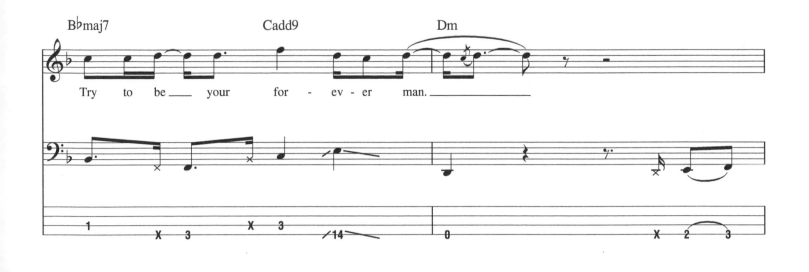

Try to be ___ your for - ev - er man. _____

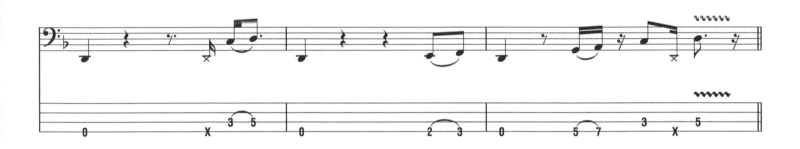

Guitar Solo

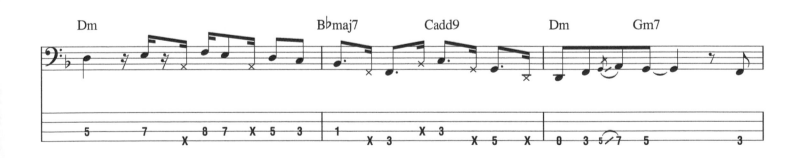

Dm

Verse
B♭maj7   Cadd9   Dm

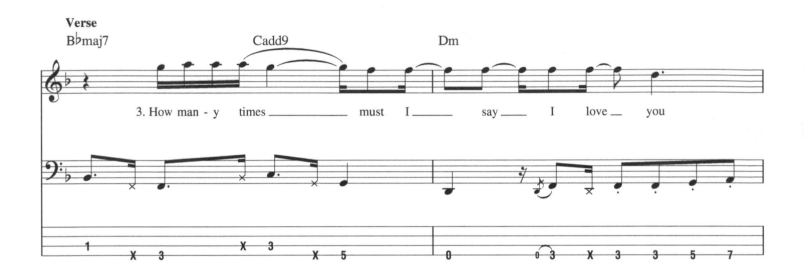

3. How man - y times _____ must I _____ say ___ I love ___ you

B♭maj7   Cadd9   Dm

'fore you fi - n'ly un - der - stand? _____

B♭maj7   Cadd9   Dm   Gm7

Won't you be ___ my for - ev - er wom - an? _____

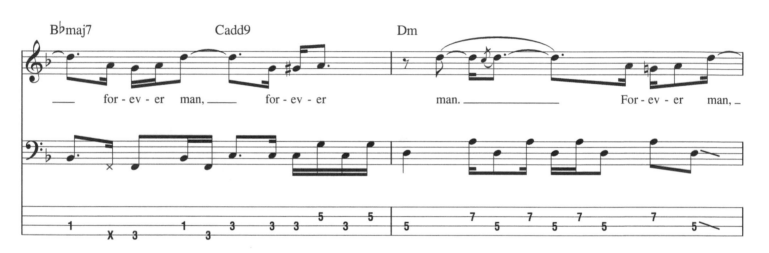

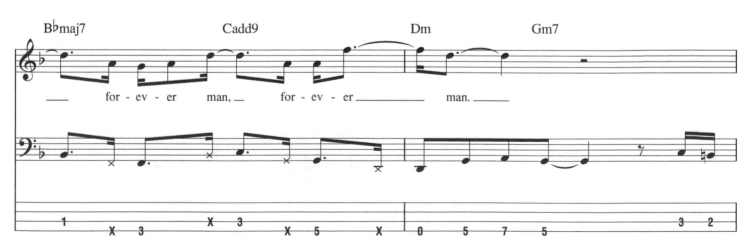

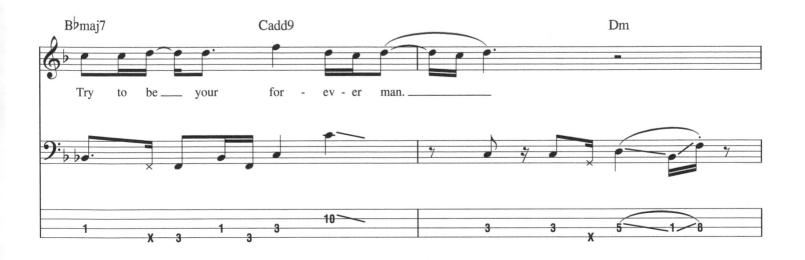

Try to be — your for - ev - er man. —

Outro-Guitar Solo

N.C.(Dm)

Begin fade   *Fade out*

I Shot the Sheriff

Words and Music by Bob Marley

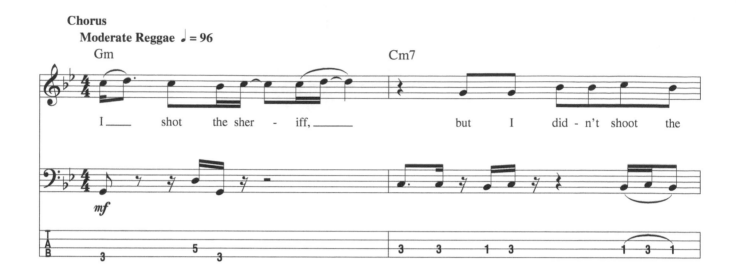

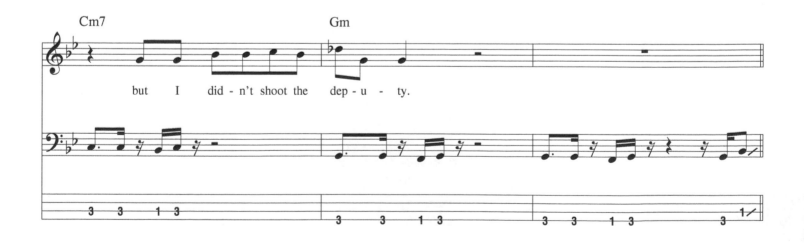

ty. _____ But I say: ___

Chorus

I ___ shot the sher - iff, _____ but I swear it was in self - de - fense.

I ___ shot the sher - iff, _____ and they say it is a

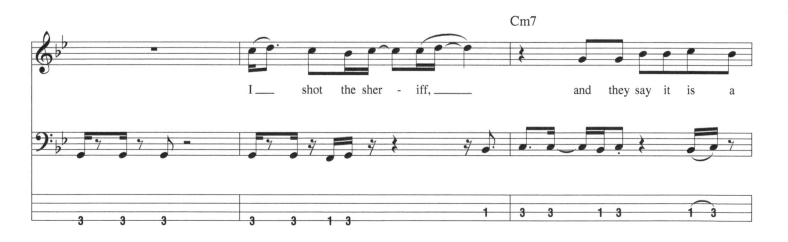

cap - i - tal of - fense.

Verse

2. Sher - iff ___ John __ Brown

34

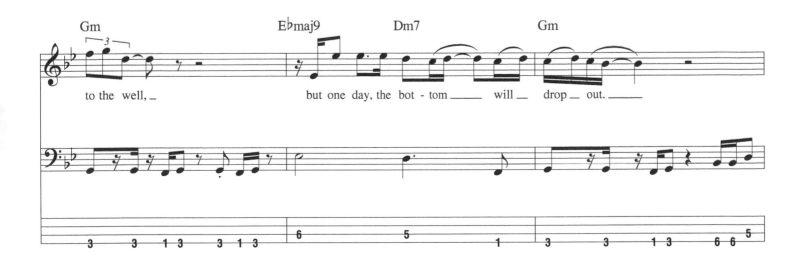

to the well, _ but one day, the bot - tom ___ will ___ drop __ out. ___

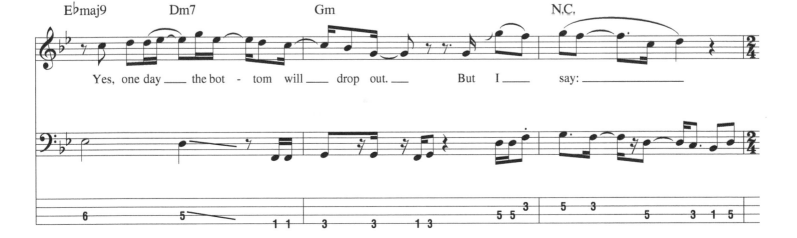

Yes, one day ___ the bot - tom will ___ drop __ out. ___ But I ___ say: _____

D.S. al Coda

⊕ **Coda**

Repeat and fade

Outro

dep - u - ty, ___ oh ___ no. ___

Lay Down Sally

Words and Music by Eric Clapton, Marcy Levy and George Terry

Don't you think ___ you want ___ some - one ___ to talk ___ to?

Lay down Sal - ly, ___ no

need to leave ___ so soon. ___ I've been try - ing all ___

___ night long ___ just to talk to you. ___

Verse

2. The sun ain't near-ly on ____ the rise, ____ and we still got ____ the moon ____ and stars ____ a - bove. ____

Un - der - neath ____ the vel - vet skies, ____

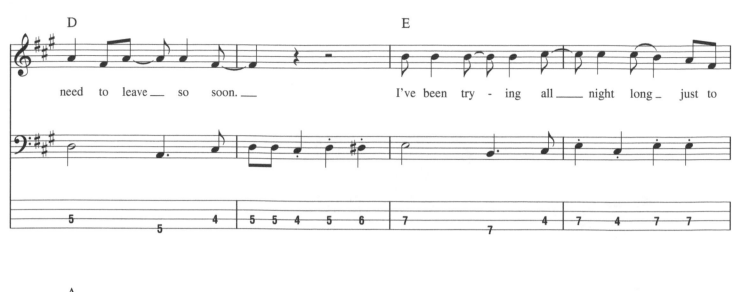

need to leave __ so soon. __   I've been try - ing all __ night long __ just to

talk to you. __   Lay down Sal - ly,   and

rest here in __ my arms. __   Don't you think __ you want __ some - one __ to talk __

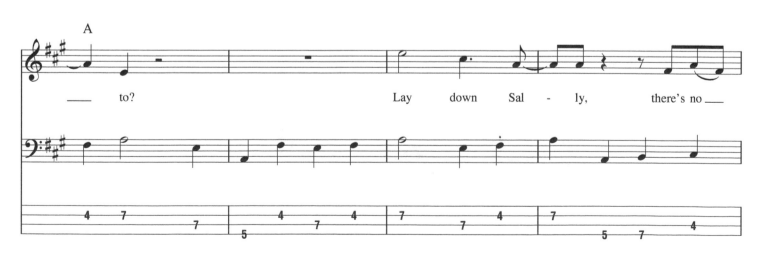

__ to?   Lay down Sal - ly,   there's no __

need to leave __ so soon. __ I've been try - ing all __

night long __ just to talk to you. __

Outro

Begin fade

Fade out

Layla

Words and Music by Eric Clapton and Jim Gordon

1. Ah, what -'ll you do __ when you get lone - ly,
2., 3. *See additional lyrics*

and no - bod - y's wait - in' by your __ side?

You been run - nin' and

la, _____ you got me on _____ my knees. _____ Lay -
(Lay - la. _____)

I'm beg - gin', dar - lin', please. _____ Lay - la, _____
la. _____

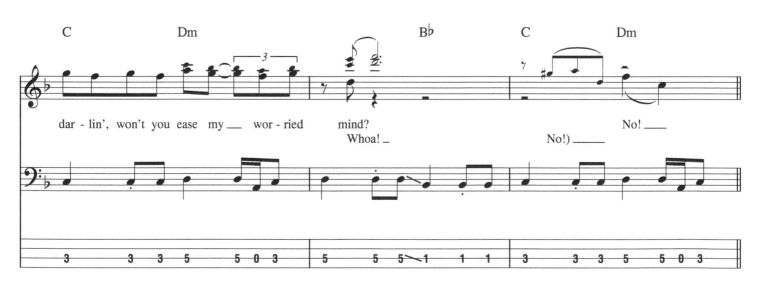

dar - lin', won't you ease my _____ wor - ried mind? No! _____
Whoa! _ No!) _____

Guitar Solo

Play 11 times

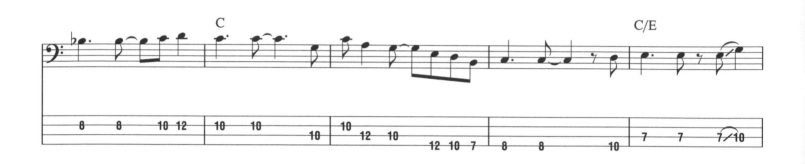

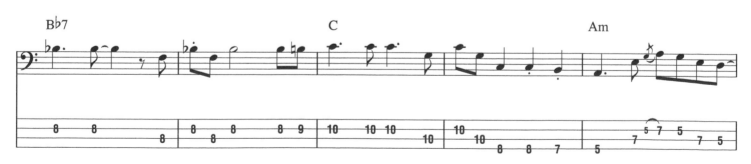

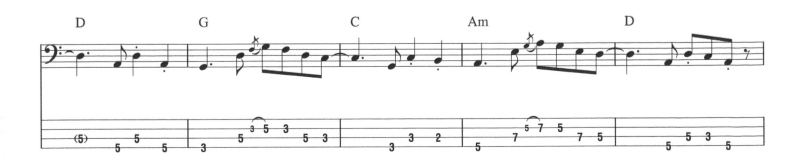

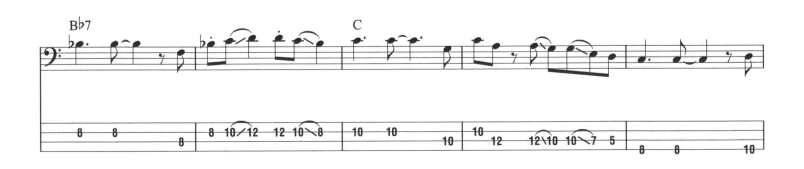

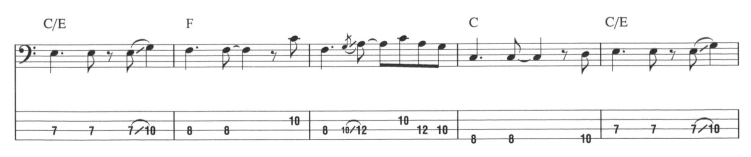

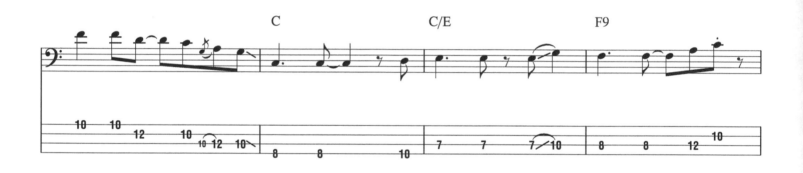

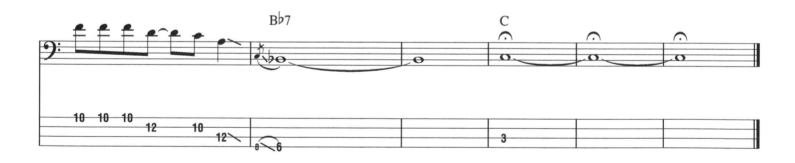

Additional Lyrics

2. I tried to give you consolation
   When your old man, he let you down.
   Like a fool, I fell in love with you,
   You turned my whole world upside down.

3. So make the best of the situation,
   Before I finally go insane.
   Please don't say we'll never find a way,
   And tell me all my love's in vain.

Wonderful Tonight

Words and Music by Eric Clapton

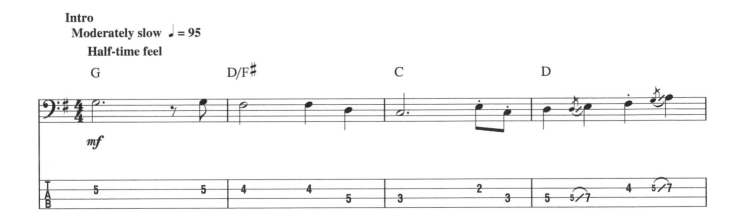

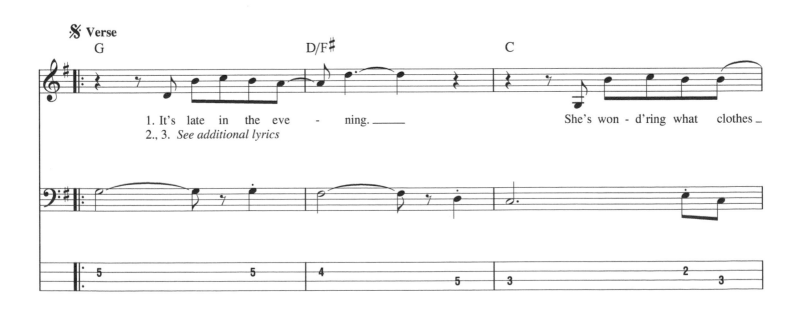

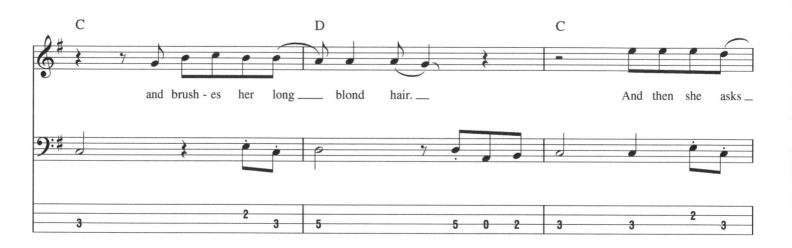

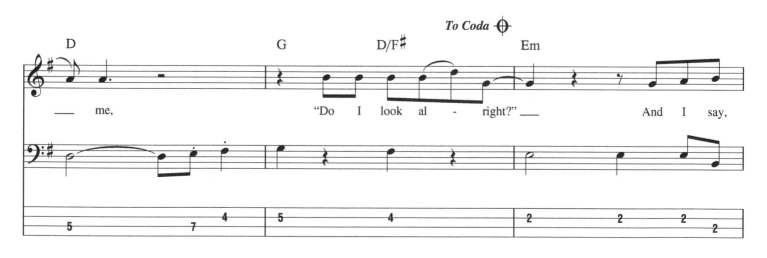

won - der - ful ____ to - night." ___

Bridge

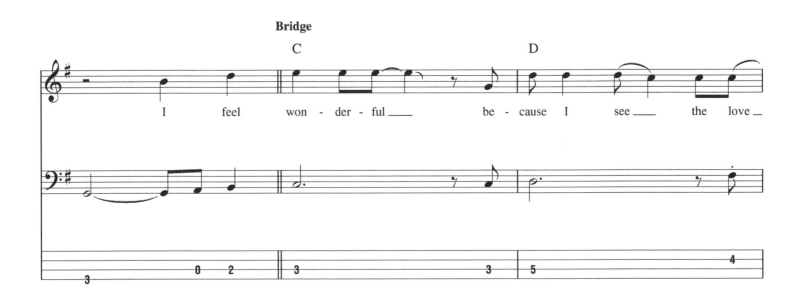

I feel won - der - ful ____ be - cause I see ____ the love ___

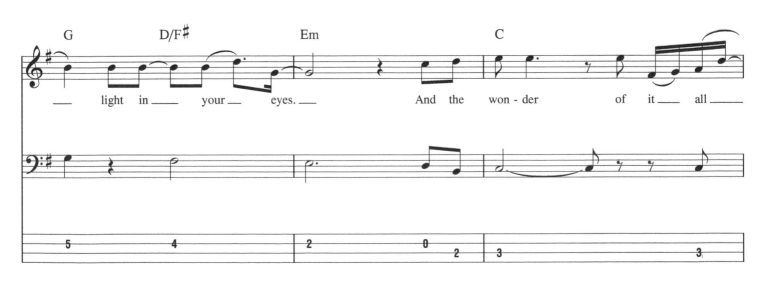

____ light in ____ your ____ eyes. ___ And the won - der of it ____ all ____

is that you just don't _ re - al - ize _ how _ much _ I love _

Interlude

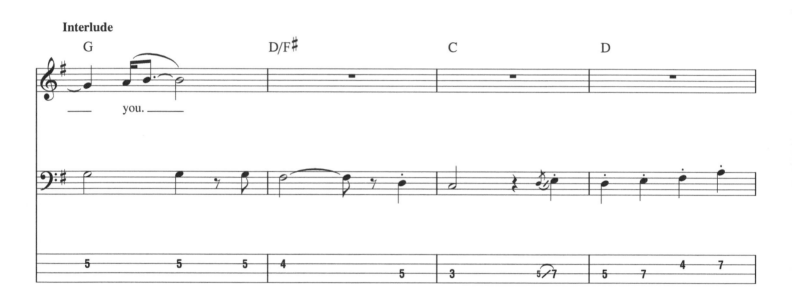

_ you. _

D.S. al Coda

Coda

And I say, "Yes, I _ feel won - der - ful _ to - night." _

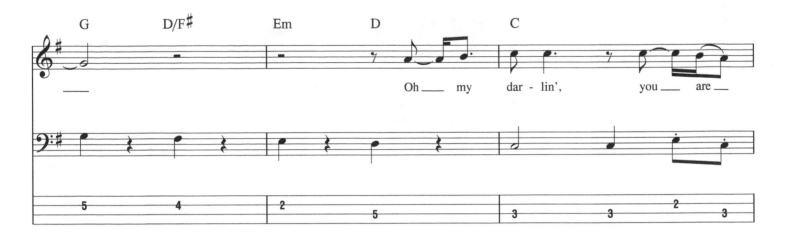

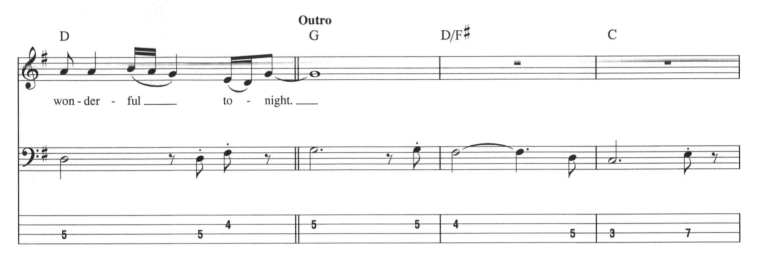

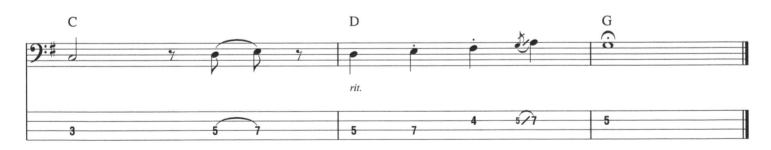

Additional lyrics

2. We go to a party, and ev'ryone turns to see
   This beautiful lady that's walking around with me.
   And then she asks me, "Do you feel alright?"
   And I say, "Yes, I feel wonderful tonight."

3. It's time to go home now, and I've got an aching head.
   So I give her the car keys and she helps me to bed.
   And then I tell her, as I turn out the light,
   I say, "My darling, you are wonderful tonight."

HAL•LEONARD® BASS PLAY-ALONG

The Bass Play-Along™ Series will help you play your favorite songs quickly and easily! Just follow the tab, listen to the audio to hear how the bass should sound, and then play-along using the separate backing tracks. The melody and lyrics are also included in the book in case you want to sing, or to simply help you follow along. The audio files are enhanced so you can adjust the recording to any tempo without changing pitch!

1. Rock
00699674 Book/Online Audio $16.99

2. R&B
00699675 Book/Online Audio $15.99

3. Pop/Rock
00699677 Book/Online Audio $16.99

4. '90s Rock
00699677 Book/Online Audio $16.99

5. Funk
00699680 Book/Online Audio $16.99

6. Classic Rock
00699678 Book/Online Audio $17.99

8. Punk Rock
00699813 Book/CD Pack $12.95

9. Blues
00699817 Book/Online Audio $16.99

10. Jimi Hendrix – Smash Hits
00699815 Book/Online Audio $17.99

11. Country
00699818 Book/CD Pack $12.95

12. Punk Classics
00699814 Book/CD Pack $12.99

13. The Beatles
00275504 Book/Online Audio $16.99

14. Modern Rock
00699821 Book/CD Pack $14.99

15. Mainstream Rock
00699822 Book/CD Pack $14.99

16. '80s Metal
00699825 Book/CD Pack $16.99

17. Pop Metal
00699826 Book/CD Pack $14.99

18. Blues Rock
00699828 Book/CD Pack $16.99

19. Steely Dan
00700203 Book/Online Audio $16.99

20. The Police
00700270 Book/Online Audio $19.99

21. Metallica: 1983-1988
00234338 Book/Online Audio $19.99

22. Metallica: 1991-2016
00234339 Book/Online Audio $19.99

**23. Pink Floyd –
Dark Side of The Moon**
00700847 Book/Online Audio $15.99

24. Weezer
00700960 Book/CD Pack $14.99

25. Nirvana
00701047 Book/Online Audio $17.99

26. Black Sabbath
00701180 Book/Online Audio $16.99

27. Kiss
00701181 Book/Online Audio $16.99

28. The Who
00701182 Book/Online Audio $19.99

29. Eric Clapton
00701183 Book/Online Audio $15.99

30. Early Rock
00701184 Book/CD Pack $15.99

31. The 1970s
00701185 Book/CD Pack $14.99

32. Cover Band Hits
00211598 Book/Online Audio $16.99

33. Christmas Hits
00701197 Book/CD Pack $12.99

34. Easy Songs
00701480 Book/Online Audio $16.99

35. Bob Marley
00701702 Book/Online Audio $17.99

36. Aerosmith
00701886 Book/CD Pack $14.99

37. Modern Worship
00701920 Book/Online Audio $17.99

38. Avenged Sevenfold
00702386 Book/CD Pack $16.99

39. Queen
00702387 Book/Online Audio $16.99

40. AC/DC
14041594 Book/Online Audio $16.99

41. U2
00702582 Book/Online Audio $16.99

42. Red Hot Chili Peppers
00702991 Book/Online Audio $19.99

43. Paul McCartney
00703079 Book/Online Audio $17.99

44. Megadeth
00703080 Book/CD Pack $16.99

45. Slipknot
00703201 Book/CD Pack $16.99

46. Best Bass Lines Ever
00103359 Book/Online Audio $19.99

47. Dream Theater
00111940 Book/Online Audio $24.99

48. James Brown
00117421 Book/CD Pack $16.99

49. Eagles
00119936 Book/Online Audio $17.99

50. Jaco Pastorius
00128407 Book/Online Audio $17.99

51. Stevie Ray Vaughan
00146154 Book/CD Pack $16.99

52. Cream
00146159 Book/Online Audio $17.99

56. Bob Seger
00275503 Book/Online Audio $16.99

57. Iron Maiden
00278398 Book/Online Audio $17.99

58. Southern Rock
00278436 Book/Online Audio $17.99

HAL•LEONARD®

Prices, contents, and availability subject to change without notice.

Visit Hal Leonard Online at **www.halleonard.com**

BASS RECORDED VERSIONS

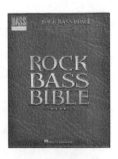

Bass Recorded Versions feature authentic transcriptions written in standard notation and tablature for bass guitar. This series features complete bass lines from the classics to contemporary superstars.

25 Essential Rock Bass Classics
00690210 / $17.99

Aerosmith – Bass Collection
00690413 / $17.95

Avenged Sevenfold – Nightmare
00691054 / $19.99

The Beatles – Abbey Road
00128336 / $22.99

The Beatles – 1962-1966
00690556 / $19.99

The Beatles – 1967-1970
00690557 / $22.99

Best of Bass Tab
00141806 / $15.99

The Best of Blink 182
00690549 / $18.95

Blues Bass Classics
00690291 / $17.99

Boston – Bass Collection
00690935 / $19.95

Stanley Clarke – Collection
00672307 / $19.99

Dream Theater – Bass Anthology
00119345 / $24.99

Funk Bass Bible
00690744 / $24.99

Hard Rock Bass Bible
00690746 / $19.99

**Jimi Hendrix –
Are You Experienced?**
00690371 / $17.95

Jimi Hendrix – Bass Tab Collection
00160505 / $22.99

Iron Maiden – Bass Anthology
00690867 / $22.99

Jazz Bass Classics
00102070 / $19.99

The Best of Kiss
00690080 / $19.99

**Lynyrd Skynyrd –
All-Time Greatest Hits**
00690956 / $22.99

Bob Marley – Bass Collection
00690568 / $19.99

Mastodon – Crack the Skye
00691007 / $19.99

Megadeth – Bass Anthology
00691191 / $22.99

Metal Bass Tabs
00103358 / $19.99

Best of Marcus Miller
00690811 / $24.99

Motown Bass Classics
00690253 / $16.99

Muse – Bass Tab Collection
00123275 / $19.99

Nirvana – Bass Collection
00690066 / $19.99

No Doubt – Tragic Kingdom
00120112 / $22.95

**Nothing More –
Guitar & Bass Collection**
0065439 / $24.99

The Offspring – Greatest Hits
00690809 / $17.95

The Essential Jaco Pastorius
00690420 / $19.99

**Jaco Pastorius –
Greatest Jazz Fusion Bass Player**
00690421 / $19.99

Pearl Jam – Ten
00694882 / $19.99

Pink Floyd – Dark Side of the Moon
00660172 / $15.99

The Best of Police
00660207 / $19.99

Pop/Rock Bass Bible
00690747 / $17.95

Queen – The Bass Collection
00690065 / $19.99

R&B Bass Bible
00690745 / $22.99

Rage Against the Machine
00690248 / $19.99

**Red Hot Chili Peppers –
BloodSugarSexMagik**
00690064 / $19.99

**Red Hot Chili Peppers –
By the Way**
00690585 / $22.99

**Red Hot Chili Peppers –
Californication**
00690390 / $19.99

**Red Hot Chili Peppers –
Greatest Hits**
00690675 / $19.99

**Red Hot Chili Peppers –
I'm with You**
00691167 / $22.99

**Red Hot Chili Peppers –
One Hot Minute**
00690091 / $19.99

**Red Hot Chili Peppers –
Stadium Arcadium**
00690853 / Book Only $24.95
00690863 / Book/CD $39.95

Rock Bass Bible
00690446 / $19.99

Rolling Stones – Bass Collection
00690256 / $19.99

Royal Blood
00151826 / $22.99

**Rush – The Spirit of Radio:
Greatest Hits 1974-1987**
00323856 / $22.99

Best of Billy Sheehan
00173972 / $24.99

Slap Bass Bible
00159716 / $24.99

Sly & The Family Stone for Bass
00109733 / $19.99

Best of Yes
00103044 / $4.99

Best of ZZ Top for Bass
00691069 / $22.99

HAL•LEONARD®

Visit Hal Leonard Online at
www.halleonard.com

BASS BUILDERS

A series of technique book/audio packages created for the purposeful building and development of your chops. Each volume is written by an expert in that particular technique. And with the inclusion of audio, the added dimension of hearing exactly how to play particular grooves and techniques make these truly like private lessons.

BASS FOR BEGINNERS
by Glenn Letsch
00695099 Book/CD Pack......................... $19.95

BASS GROOVES
by Jon Liebman
00696028 Book/Online Audio $19.99

BASS IMPROVISATION
by Ed Friedland
00695164 Book/Online Audio $19.99

BLUES BASS
by Jon Liebman
00695235 Book/Online Audio $19.99

BUILDING WALKING BASS LINES
by Ed Friedland
00695008 Book/Online Audio $19.99

RON CARTER – BUILDING JAZZ BASS LINES
00841240 Book/Online Audio $19.99

DICTIONARY OF BASS GROOVES
by Sean Malone
00695266 Book/Online Audio $14.95

EXPANDING WALKING BASS LINES
by Ed Friedland
00695026 Book/Online Audio $19.99

FINGERBOARD HARMONY FOR BASS
by Gary Willis
00695043 Book/Online Audio $17.99

FUNK BASS
by Jon Liebman
00699348 Book/Online Audio $19.99

FUNK/FUSION BASS
by Jon Liebman
00696553 Book/Online Audio $24.99

HIP-HOP BASS
by Josquin des Prés
00695589 Book/Online Audio $15.99

JAZZ BASS
by Ed Friedland
00695084 Book/Online Audio $17.99

JERRY JEMMOTT – BLUES AND RHYTHM & BLUES BASS TECHNIQUE
00695176 Book/CD Pack......................... $24.99

JUMP 'N' BLUES BASS
by Keith Rosier
00695292 Book/Online Audio $17.99

THE LOST ART OF COUNTRY BASS
by Keith Rosier
00695107 Book/Online Audio $19.99

PENTATONIC SCALES FOR BASS
by Ed Friedland
00696224 Book/Online Audio $19.99

REGGAE BASS
by Ed Friedland
00695163 Book/Online Audio $16.99

'70S FUNK & DISCO BASS
by Josquin des Prés
00695614 Book/Online Audio $16.99

SIMPLIFIED SIGHT-READING FOR BASS
by Josquin des Prés
00695085 Book/Online Audio $17.99

6-STRING BASSICS
by David Gross
00695221 Book/Online Audio $14.99

HAL•LEONARD®

halleonard.com

Prices, contents and availability subject to change without notice; All prices are listed in U.S. funds